HATS FOR CATS!

HATS FOR CATS!

By Christine Michael

Illustrated By:
Andy Kociuch
and
Nick Gilbert

EXPANSIONS UNLIMITED
NOTTINGHAM

First edition published: July 1996
Second edition (revised and reset)
published: May 2001
Third edition published: March 2006

Published By:
Expansions Unlimited Press
PO Box 30,
South PDO
Nottingham NG2 7JP

All rights reserved. No part of this publication
may be reproduced, stored in a retrieval system, or
transmitted in any form, or by any means, electronic,
mechanical, photocopying, recording, or otherwise,
without prior permission of the publisher.

© Christine Michael 1996, 2001, 2006

Reprinted 2007

ISBN: 978-1-900410-35-9

Printed By:
Proprint
Remus House
Coltsfoot Drive
Woodston
PE2 9JX

INTRODUCTION

I have used the poem **'Hats for Cats'** when doing workshops, assemblies and lessons with young people in England and in Germany. It's fascinating to hear the German translation of it! It's one of those poems that often seems to inspire youngsters to write something of their own which is an aspect of my work that I'm keen to help with. In a way, everyone is a poet and poetry should have something to do with sharing, caring and creating a better world.

Now that Angiy is grown-up she doesn't have a bedroom here to stick up pictures and poems but hope that you will continue to put displays up in your schools and libraries. Let me know how you are getting on with your writing and drawings.

http://www.geocities.com/christinemichael

ACKNOWLEDGEMENTS

'Hats for Cats' first appeared in one of the Open University Poet's Association magazines and a copy was apparently sent off to Her Majesty at the Palace! It also appeared in the volume of poems *New Faces* published by Bradgate Press plus Martin Glynn and David Orme used it in an anthology of poems called ***'Doin Mi Ead'*** published by Piper.

I would like to thank Ann Fairbairn of the Education Library Services in Nottingham for the help she has given me in obtaining work with youngsters. I would also like to thank Hilary Parker and Claudia Eckert for the translation of the poem into German and to my friends who organised the Interlese in Magdeburg, particularly Dorothea Iser, for enabling me to perform the poem in and around Magdeburg and to Regine Kress-Fricke of Karlsruhe for her help and encouragement.

I would also like to thank my son Derek for inspiring me in the first place to write the original Hats for Cats poem and for his and my daughter Angiy's support and useful comments plus the help of Andy Kociuch and Nick Gilbert for illustrating so well.

This book is dedicated to all the young people that I have worked with, for those adults I have worked with who are young at heart and for all of those to come!

CONTENTS

A Clumsy Poem	1
Asking About Assonance	2
Blindness	3
Billy Beansprout	4
Candy Man	5
Child's Picture Gallery	7
Eh-sha	8
Hold my Hand and Shake it Now	9
Ghosties and Things	10
Hats for Cats!	12
How Do I Write a Poem?	14
If I Were ...	15
I'm Gonna Sing to Make You Happy!	17
I Invented a Word	18
If Words Were Made of Candyfloss	20
I Think the World is Magic	21
Lines for Luvers	22
Lingo's	23
Listen to the Beat	24
Making Things Rhyme	25
Met a phor	26
My Dad's Got an Eye at the Back of his Head	27
Patter	27
My Mate's an Alien	28
Our Cat Thinks She's a Cow!	29
Parks	30
Robin Hood Song	32
Shirley's Theory	35

Sill i bulls!	36
Strive for a Better World	37
Some Similes	38
Space Is ...	40
The Journeys of Lata	41
There's a Wind That Whistles	43
Things in my Bedclothes	44
The Disappearance	45
Witchy Winklestopper	48
The Whole World is a Garden	50
WarWords!	52
When Mum Fell Down the Plug-Hole!	53
Angiy Michael's page	56
My Friend Fred	57
Tongue Twisters	58
Our Ghost Is Very Polite	59
Six Weeks	60
If I Were At The Seaside	62
Percy And The Pirates	64
Percy In The Washing Machine	66
Percy And Popsy	68
Will You . . .?	70
Fried Eggs And Jam	72
In August	74
There Are Aliens In My Classroom	76
There Are Things In My Room At Night	78
Light Haikus	80

A CLUMSY POEM

I will clumsily write myself a poem
in language loose as days
a jelly of a poem plopped
on a plate from a mould manufactured
out of plastic
sure as industry.
My jelly poem will wobble
topped by ice-cream
frozen for a moment
like language
in an era
that forgets
about melting moments
and mixing
the transparency of words
jargonned for control
the power of setting
words held together
by molecules of meaning
gelled coloured
flavoured
for instant delight!

ASKING ABOUT ASSONANCE

Asking about assonance
Announcements were made
Allowing additional factors
About language to be portrayed.

As we are asking about assonance today
Let's enclose entries enveloped
Ready to say!

Every echo of sound
Every inch of inclusion
In the words that we use
Represent fusion
Of feelings realised
Through thoughts
Oh so open
Utterances of moments,
Moments we're hoping
To lift into infinite possibilities
Rhythms, implications
And intricate minutes.

So take a and e
And i, o and u
Play with their magic
see what they do!

BLINDNESS

Thick grey matter
Mass of atoms
Swirling
Twirling
Blinding
Fog

From out the muted air
I was touched
Taken by the arm
And led
Safely home
To bed

So the blind
Led the blind
And I see
Far more
Than I saw
Before

BILLY BEANSPROUT

Billy Beansprout put beans in his ears
Though his mother had told him and so had his peers
That the danger of placing such objects in there
Would bring consequences one wouldn't dare
To imagine, so imagine we will
Just think, just sit still...

Beans in your ears!
What could they grow into
Why peppers, courgettes?!
You'd hardly begin to
Visualise the possibilities!
Apple trees, plum trees,
Oranges and pears!
Walking down the road
People would stare!

So never put beans in your ears for a dare
You could turn into a gooseberry bush sitting on a chair!
Billy Beansprout was actually put on display
With all the Spring flowers
In the month of May!

CANDYMAN

The man with the basket
Is coming down our street
Calling out to all of us
'Come buy my sweets.'

We run and we plead
With our Mums to lend
Us lots of pocket money
So we can spend

Our money on candy
So lovely and luscious
Making mouths water
For the ones we find delicious.

Sometimes our Mothers
Can't afford
We must wait for Dad
To come home from abroad.

For Dad's in the Navy
Earning the dosh
To bring home to Mum
So we can be posh!!!

Eat too many sweets
You'll get a double chin
It happened to a girl
Who used to be thin

Too much sugar candy
Makes your teeth go bad
But we still look forward
To seeing our Dad!!!

CHILD'S PICTURE GALLERY

Two boxers with red gloves
and boots - macho chests
tough mouths - a bird in flight
towards the sun - a girl
in a red dress between
two unreal but beautiful
flowers - the face of a child
with eyes like eggs - the captured curve
of a snail framed
by yellow hair - a still-life drawing
of crayons and pencils
in pots - a dracula face
passionate tongue dripping
anticipation between
two unlikely tusks
a demure clown in braces
holding rectangular trousers
a butterfly bigger than the sun
an owl stunned by stars
a ship with visible anchor
an innocent blue-eyed doodle dog
a stubby-legged horse
embedded in abundant
obedient grass - an orange cat
with green whiskers - a rainbow
with distinct colours in clear lines
a tortoise - friendly-faced lion
orange-maned to match the sun
fish sinking below curved waves.....

EH-SHA

Eh-sha
Eh-sha
Eh-sha
Eh-sha
Imma-mamma
Imma-mamma
Imma-mamma
Imma-mamma

Tag-tag-ta
Tag-tag-ta
Tag-tag-ta
Tag-tag-ta

Eh-sha Eh-sha Eh-sha Eh-sha
Imma-mamma Imma-mamma Imma-mamma Imma-mamma
Tag-tag-ta Tag-tag-ta Tag-tag-ta Tag-tag-ta

HOLD MY HAND AND SHAKE IT NOW

Hold my hand and shake it now
Let's sing a song both soft and loud
We'll all sing together hand in hand
We'll all be friends from different lands.

We'll all be together
Singing a lovely song
Shaking hands
The whole day long!

Let's sing of peace, kindness and love
Let's sing of harmony, rising above
Unkindness and hatred and things that cause pain
Let's all shake hands again and again!

GHOSTIES AND THINGS

The ghost who came to haunt me
Had his hat on all crooked
He was obviously unaware
Of the way he looked.

His whiteness was peculiar too
It was done up with buttons
All askew!

We've got a ghost who goes to the loo
At 12 o'clock, 1 o'clock
And half-past 2!

Our ghost's bigger than your ghost
Na nani nana
It's not as big as your Dad though!

Our ghost's got an eye on the end of its finger
It pokes it round the door at night and says:
'Eye! eye!
Just looking in Sir!'

HATS FOR CATS!

I was walking down the road on my way to school
When I met these cats playing the fool
They were dancing on the pavement
spinning n their backs
And all of them were wearing hats
They were singing a song which sounded like a rap
And the song they sang was **HATS FOR CATS!**
HATS FOR CATS MAN HATS FOR CATS!
The name of the song is **HATS FOR CATS!**
I stood on the corner listening to the rap
When they saw me there in my old school cap
They said 'join in the fun boy, join in the fun
This singing and a ringing has just begun'
We were popping and a bopping all the way to school
Everyone we passed thought us real cool
The headmaster was standing in his cap and gown
When he saw us coming he gave us a frown
But he listened to us - then joined in
You should have seen him doing that spin!
The teachers and the children they had a ball
Moonwalking in the assembly hall
HATS FOR CATS MAN! HATS FOR CATS!
The name of the song is **HATS FOR CATS!**
The BBC heard about us
We went on TV and we caused quite a fuss
The news media they came around
And everybody joined in the sound
Soon the nation was a'singing as they joined in the beat
Even Mr Blair found his feet!

We went to the Palace, the guards were in a line
Spinning and a popping all dressed so fine
My friend Tabby he looked at the Queen
He said 'Queenie Queenie where have you been?'
She looked back at him - put on her crown
Then she began spinning around
She said - **'WAVE!'**
We said - **'WAVE!'**
HATS FOR CATS MAN! HATS FOR CATS!
The name of the song is **HATS FOR CATS!**
Various nations sent their spies
They could hardly believe their eyes
News got around that the world was a spinning
Everybody in the world was a dancing and a singing
We sang **PEACE!**
We sang **LOVE!**
HATS FOR CATS MAN! HATS FOR CATS!
Everybody sing **HATS FOR CATS!**

HOW DO I WRITE A POEM?

How do I write a poem?
Open my mind
Write down some thoughts

Draw some pictures
Of things I've been taught

Ideas I soon find

Writing down words
Rhyming them in my head
If they won't rhyme
Tapping beats instead to
Each word said

Adding rhythm to the lines

Poems are fun
Often beating in time
Each poem I write is
Mine!

IF I WERE

If I were a flower
I would be
A daisy near
An apple tree -
So I could see
Blossom in the Spring
And laugh with the birds
As they come out to sing.

If I were a bird
I'd be a swan
Black and graceful -
A royal one
With a crown on my head
I'd be kind and true
And fly to strange lands
Starting life anew.

If I were an animal
I'd be a unicorn
Hiding in forests
I'd come out at dawn
I'd weave magic and laughter
And send a sweet dove
On a mysterious rainbow
To the world - with love!

I'M GONNA SING TO MAKE YOU HAPPY!

I'm gonna sing to make you happy
I'm gonna sing to make you happy
I'm gonna sing to make you happy
So spread that happiness around.

We're gonna sing to make our teachers happy
We're gonna sing to make our teachers happy
We're gonna sing to make our teachers happy
So spread that happiness around.

We're gonna sing to make our mummies happy
We're gonna sing to make our mummies happy
We're gonna sing to make our mummies happy
So spread that happiness around.

We're gonna sing to make our daddies happy
We're gonna sing to make our daddies happy
We're gonna sing to make our daddies happy
So spread that happiness around.

We're gonna sing to make each other happy
We're gonna sing to make each other happy
We're gonna sing to make each other happy
So spread that happiness around.

(Add your own verses!)

I INVENTED A WORD

I invented a word
It said: 'Oojingfingfedgebottomsideways!'
I said 'Would you like a cup of tea?'
It said: 'Oojingfingfedgebottomsideways!'
It drank it's tea
And said: 'Oojingfingfedgebottomsideways?'
Mum made breakfast
The word said: 'Oojingfingfedgebottomsideways!'
Mum said: 'Okay'
And had a cup of tea!

I took the word to school
The word said: 'Oojingfingfedgebottomsideways!'
My friends said: 'What's that you said?'
The word said: 'Oojingfingfedgebottomsideways!'
So we played with it in the playground.

The bell rang
The word said: 'Oojingfingfedgebottomsideways!'
The bell answered it
And said: 'Ring, ring, ring!'
The word said: 'Oojingfingfedgebottomsideways!'

We went to Assembly
The headteacher said 'Good morning everybody'
The word said: 'Oojingfingfedgebottomsideways!'
Everyone began to sing and swing!

We went to write poems
The word said: 'Oojingfingfedgebottomsideways'
I made a poem out of it!

IF WORDS WERE MADE OF CANDYFLOSS

If words were made of candyfloss
And capitals ice-cream
Punctuation made of nutty fudge
Paragraphs - a chocolate dream!

Then when we wrote our poems
We would have a lovely time
With all these delicious words
We'd make the sweetest rhyme!

I THINK THE WORLD IS MAGIC

I think the world is magic
Just because it's there
So many things to look at
So many things to share.

Magic could help me listen
If I could not see
When stars and moon glisten
They would speak to me.

Magic could help me see so well
If I could not hear
So many wonderful colours
And all so crystal clear.

Magic helps me smell and taste
Touch textures coarse and fine
I think the world is magic
For it's yours and mine!

LINES FOR LUVERS

Thou art more lovely than
A sausage in a frying pan!

My luv is like a red red rose
It's a bit like Rudolf Reindeer's nose!

My luv's wicked my luv's cool
I'm her man so she's no fool!

I luv toffee I luv jam
But most of all
I luv my Mam!

Luveo luveo wherefore art thou luveo?
I'm helpin' me dad to give the car a shuveo!

LINGO'S

There are many different lingo's
Around the world
Many ways of saying things
Many words to learn.

Sounds
Speaking
Sharing
Greeting
Reaching

'Hello'
'How do you do?'
'Sava'
'Comment 'allez vous'

Friendships
In the making
Breaking
The silences

'Guten tag'
'Nameste'
'A salaam a lachem'
'Sasrigar'
'Caed mile failte'
'Shalom'

We share them all
In this world our home.

LISTEN TO THE BEAT

If you're not so good at Mathematics
And no-one seems very sympathetic
Play that music - go hip-hop
You'll be going right to the top!
You must - listen to the beat listen to the beat
Loosen your body and tap your feet
Go with the Rhythm - relax your mind
Swing to the time and you will find
That counting comes quite naturally
It's as simple as ABC!

Tell your teacher all about it
Let your class begin to shout it
Listen to the beat listen to the beat
Loosen your body and tap your feet
1234 - count again
See if you can get to 10
How many patterns can you find
Spinning their way through your mind
As you - listen to the beat listen to the beat
Loosen your body and tap your feet
Count at home count on the street
Listen to the beat listen to the beat....

MAKING THINGS RHYME

Making things rhyme
They don't have to you know
Let words follow time
And go with the flow
If you really want to rhyme
The words you are using
Make your own book
And if words are refusing
To find partners in crime
Then go through the alphabet
Dictionary and thesaurus
Don't be afraid of the word 'brontosaurus'
Build up your lists
Of words sounding same
Join in with friends
And make it a game -
But if words want to flow, let them grow, echo,
Evolve, arrest images
Blend them easily together,
Feel rhythms pounding
Like the beat of your heart
Words pulsating with memories and possibilities
Opening universal doors
Kaleidoscopic and magnificent
Sure in their footsteps
And in your
Wonderful imagination!

MET A PHOR

Met a phor
It said: 'I'm a door
An opening
A crack
A way through
A cupboard
At the back
Of your mind
Step through me
And you will find
Scenery
Beyond compare....
If you dare!'

MY DAD'S GOT AN EYE AT THE BACK OF HIS HEAD

My dad's got an eye at the back of his head
He always knows when my brother Fred
Is getting up to some of his tricks
My dad gets him in a fix
And sends him up to bed at six!

Mum's got an eye on the end of her finger
She looks round the door when her finger lingers
She knows when my bedroom's a bit of a disgrace
She says, without coming in, 'Tidy up this place.'
How does she do it when I can't see her face?

PATTER

The explosive patter of repetitive
Tappings - loud, long, languorous, living
Things .... weeping, wondering,
Widening our minds
To the numerous murmurs
And moanings, the magic words
The music of literature.

Meanings merge into moments
Become models of possibilities
Pass through and then into
The surging, surfing, endless
Ride of rhythms and beats
Blending life's learnings longingly.

MY MATE'S AN ALIEN

My mate's an alien
He comes to school with Damien
He climbs up trees
Looking for bees
And plays the saxaphonium!

OUR CAT THINKS SHE'S A COW

Our cat thinks she's a cow
She doesn't say 'mee-ow'
She says **'MOO!'**

PARKS

Places to hide
Places to play
Places to picnic in
All through the day
Places to look at statues
Places to study trees
Places to smell the flowers
But avoid the bees
Places to go on slides
And the swings
Places with castles
But without a king
Places to feed the ducks
Places to watch deer
Places to go on roundabouts
Till everything goes queer
Parks with old building
And mazes to explore
Are really quite exciting
If you find a magic door....
It's the door of the imagination
That really helps you see
That parks are quite incredible
Places to be!

PARKS.

ROBIN HOOD SONG

Robin Hood Robin Hood
Riding on a bus
Robin Hood Robin Hood
A Nottingham omnibus
He likes to chat
In his feathered hat
Robin Hood Robin Hood Robin Hood

When Robin was a youngster
He was a lively lad
He'd shoot his arrows everywhere
And drive his mother mad!
When sitting down to dinner
It really was a treat
Sifting little arrows
Out of mother's Sweet!

He took his bow and arrow
All the way to school
And shot them in the ear-'ole
Of anyone who was cruel
One day the chief inspector
Who'd come to visit them
Left with an arrow in his ear
And won't come back again!

And when he came to leave school
He didn't know what to do
So he went to the Corporation
And said 'How do you do'.
The man behind the desk
He said 'Now let me see -
I think we have a vacancy
On the number 43!'

One May morning quite early
Maid Marion came in style
She looked at Robin dearly
And gave him such a smile
And when she came to pay her fare
He said: 'No that's all right
But I'll meet you up the Castle grounds
At six o'clock tonight!'

The Sheriff of the City
Came to speak one day
So the people went to the market square
To listen to what he'd say
Robin he got off his bus and went to hear the chat
But accidentally shot an arrow
Through the Sheriff's hat!

Now Robin is an outlaw
In the forest green
They've even got a bus out there
Which never can be seen
And Friar Tuck and Allan a'Dale
Sing folk songs all the day
But Maid Marion and Robin
Well - you don't see them all day!

SHIRLEY'S THEORY

Shirley sat in an algebra
lesson, pondering the formulae on the blackboard
and discovered through
digression of the problem
in hand and a fairly
complex series of analytical
thoughts, that the universe
was contained within a pimple
on the end of an alien creature's
nose! 'Well bless me'; she
exclaimed, sneezing in surprise.

She didn't really like to tell the maths
teacher who possessed the profoundest pimple
in the middle of furrowed line on
his forehead. 'Pimples are relative,'
she thought, 'but then so, of course, are universes
and ours is supposedly
expanding. For every problem there is
a solution,' she sauntered, reaching
for her jotter, commencing with the problem
and working backwards or forwards
as the perspective may be.

The creature was just lifting it's arm
to examine and possibly squeeze the pimple
but fortunately Shirley had considered this
in several pages of figures before the fingers
of the said being had actually made contact
with it's nose. (All the wars in the world
were somewhat futile in the face of this!)
All things being equal Shirley reached a
remarkable conclusion. (The boys during all
this summing up were throwing paper aeroplanes
round the room, girls were doing their nails.)
Shirley sealed the pimple on the page, squaring
roots.

SILL I BULLS!

I am me
You are you!
You are such a sill i moo!

Billy's sitting writing
Mother's cooking whiting
Sally's trying kiting
Father's fighting lightning???!!!

Possible linguistic solutions
Offering potential intrusions
Dominate mountainous conclusions ???!!!

STRIVE FOR A BETTER WORLD

Imagination evolution
You can find any solution
Try ....
You can do it if you try.

Mediation contemplation
Get rid of stress
Do relaxation
Try ....
You can do it if you try.

Sow a seed see it growing
Plant a tree you'll be knowing
Life ....
Is good and given to you

Don't destroy don't throw litter
Don't close your eyes don't get bitter
Strive ....
For a better world.

SOME SIMILES

My dad's as mad as a volcano
Exploding and wild
Ranting and raving
Just like a child.

Mum's like a plum
As sweet as honey
Round and cuddly
And very funny!

My brother's as daft as sticky paper
Following me round
Always asking questions -
How silly they sound!

My sister's like a silly goon
Giggling all the day
Making sounds like sea-lions
Then going out to play!

SPACE

Space is
Between your toes
Up your nose
Their toys and yours
A momentary pause
Room to move
Time to approve
A blank sheet of paper
A skyscraper
Silence of the night
Stars shining bright
Our world and theirs
People who stare
Universes beyond
Fish in a pond
Courtesy's grace
Infinite space!

THE JOURNEYS OF LATA

Lata is magic
Round the world she scurries
Helping many people
Listening to their worries.
She helps them solve their problems
Whatever they may be.
If you should see her
Say hello from me!

In the North she met Olaf
Bewailing his lot
His brother was to be King
And would inherit the lot!
Lata reminded him
Of the music played
So he made others happy
And laughed in the shade!

In the South Uzoamaka
Was crying for her mum
And the birthday present promised
Which hadn't come.
But Lata had been
At the magic market stall
Where the mother had waited with a bracelet and ball!

In the East Su Ling
Had cried and cried
For children she'd wanted
But now was denied.
Lata had told her
That a teacher she'd be
When Su Ling heard of this
She cried out with glee.

In the West there was Sammy
Buying things for his wife
But never said he loved her
In all of his life.
Lata told him the secret
Of life sweet and true
He went home to his wife
And said **'I LOVE YOU!'**

THERE'S A WIND THAT WHISTLES

There's a wind that whistles
Round the house at night
Who's a bit of a bully -
Tries to give us a fright
With the noises he makes:

Groans and moans
And ghoulie sounds
Mischievous thing!
He doesn't scare me!

My drum and trumpet
Drown him out
As a matter of fact
I scare him away
Because he doesn't come back
During the day!

THINGS IN MY BEDCLOTHES

There are things in my bedclothes
That crawl in the night
They wake me up
And give me a fright.

Mum won't believe me
When I tell her the tale
Of the cities and people
And the hump-back whale.

It gets quite alarming
When they disturb my dreams
Bed-clothes and pillows
Are not what they seem!

THE DISAPPEARANCE

The cat
went out
and disappeared
we feared
the worst
and thought
him lost
and then
the dog
went out
as well
to seek
the cat
but we
didn't know
what he
was at
we rang
the police
they could
not help
so all
over town
we searched
around
and then
the two
bedraggled
and thin
walked in

and sat
beside
the fire
with never
a 'how -
do-you-do'
or 'sorry -
the-trouble -
we've put -
you to!'

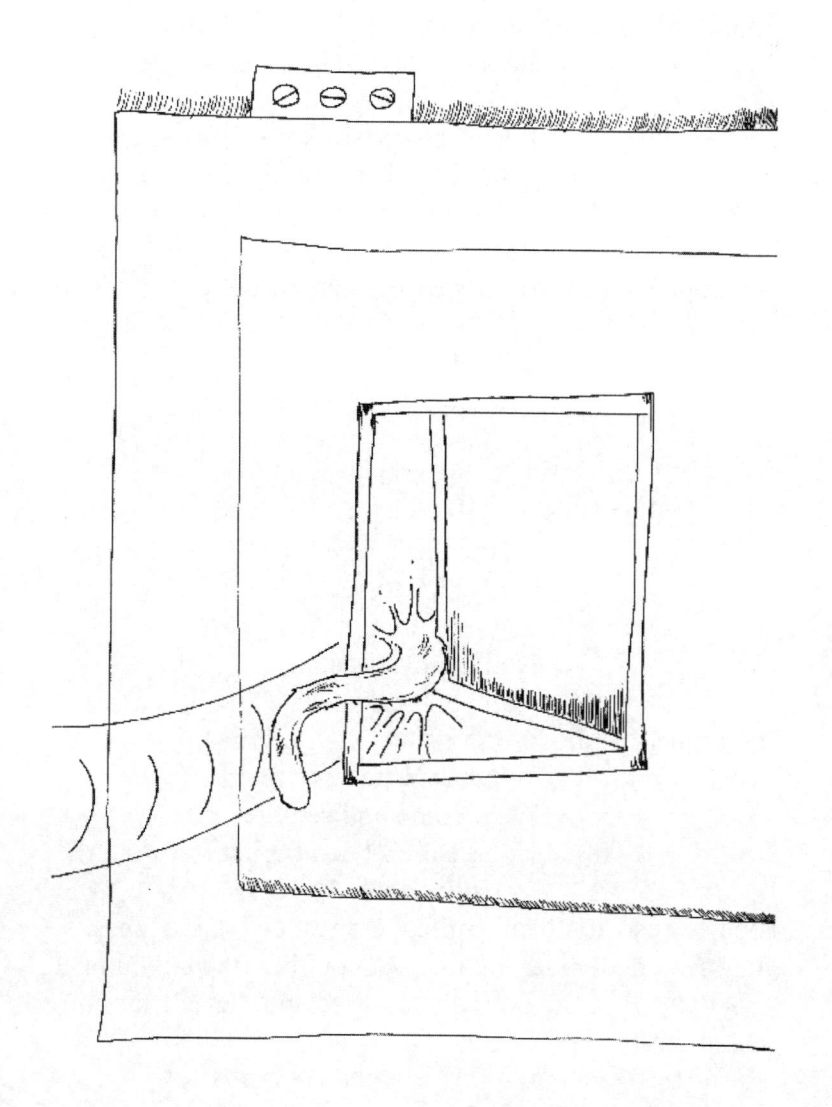

WITCHY WINKLESTOPPER

Witchy Winklestopper was getting very forgetful. She was often in a muddle these days. The other day her friend Joe had said something about treasure and told her she must look after it. Today she came out in her garden and suddenly thought: 'I've lost my treasure. Where could I have put it?'

Two rappers were passing by her garden and called out to her:
'Hey there Witchy
Is there something wrong?
Try not to worry
We'll sing you a song.'
Witchy called back:
'Hey there boys
It's nice to see
you
I've lost my treasure
Can you help me?'
The rappers replied:
'Okay Witchy
We'll come and see
If you're treasure's been buried
Under a tree.'
The tree just stood and smiled and waved it's branches. They searched under the tree but couldn't find anything so Witchy gave the boys a cup of tea and they all sat in the garden.

Two engineers came by and called:
> 'What's wrong Witchy?'

Witchy replied:
> 'I've lost my treasure
> I don't know where it's been
> I've looked around
> But it's nowhere to be seen.'

The engineers said:
> 'We'll help you find it.'

They looked round the house, near the drains, in the pipes, on the roof but they couldn't find the treasure so Witchy gave them a cup of tea and they all sat in the garden.

Joe the gardener came by and asked:
> 'What's wrong Witchy?'

Witchy replied:
> 'I've lost my treasure.
> Can you help me find it Joe?'

Joe smiled, the tree smiled, the others looked puzzled.

Joe said:
> 'The treasure that can't be measured
> Is in you
> It's your kindness
> And the things that you do.'

Witchy smiled. She remembered.

Everyone said:

'The treasure that can't be measured
Is in you
It's your kindness
And the things that you do.'

THE WHOLE WORLD IS A GARDEN

The whole world is a garden
Good and fierce
With things exposed and hidden
Thorns that pierce
Alongside gorgeous blooms.

Danger lurks but there are safe places
Quiet and still
Where you can sit and contemplate
Find them if you will.
Tread carefully and in peace.

WARWORDS!

You may call me a dandelion
You may call me a buffoon
You may call me a weed
You may call me a hot-air balloon

Your words may be painful
Your words may not be sweet
I'll have lots of words for you
Next time we meet!

But I'll keep them in my mind
Not sow them like seeds in yours
Because my words if they grow
might
EXPLODE
And cause an almighty war!!!

WHEN MUM FELL DOWN THE PLUG-HOLE!

When Mum fell down the plug-hole
It was a bit of a disaster
For a few minutes after she fell down
Dad went swimming after her!

'Oh dear' said Mum
'What shall I do?
I wanted to make
An Irish stew!'

Said Dad 'Now Darling
We've got to think
How to stop you falling
Down the kitchen sink!'

All of a sudden
They were washed out to sea
A fisherman came rowing by
And they landed on his knee!

'My word!' said Tom
This is a surprise
Never had a catch like this -
Can't believe my eyes!'

On the way to America
They met a shark
They looked inside it's mouth -
It was very dark!

On the way to China
The weather got finer
So they stopped off for tea
And telephoned me!

I was at home
Writing a poem
When the call came through
I decided what to do!

I got in my plane
Flew over the ocean
Stopped off in Spain
Got out the sun lotion!

Meanwhile Mum and Dad
Had moved to Japan
But they rang me on the mobile
Said 'Come if you can!'

I met them in India
And gave them a hug
We flew back to Nottingham
With a **GREAT BIG PLUG!**

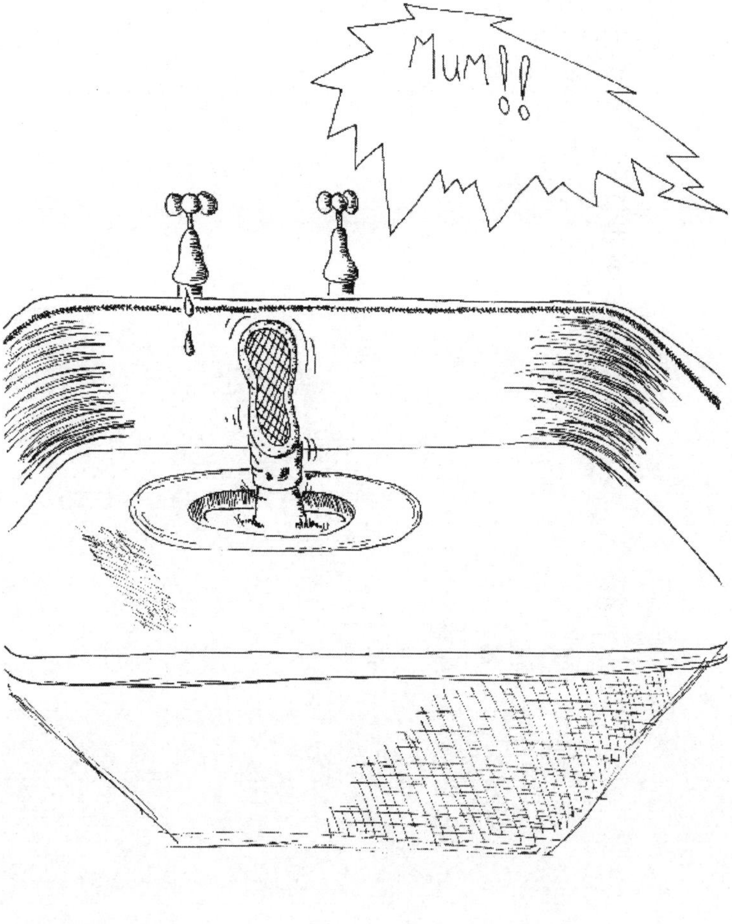
MUM!!

ANGIY MICHAEL'S PAGE

TOMMY SPROUT

Why don't you try making your own picture of Tommy Sprout?

ROBIN'S BUS.

THOU ART MORE LOVELY THAN A SAUSAGE IN A FRYING PAN

MY FRIEND FRED

My friend Fred
Has a bouncy head!
It's a bit loose too
'Cos it's missing a screw!

He plays in my room
He's a bit of a loon!
I can't stop laughing
When he plays head-passing!

He's the funniest friend
I've ever had.
He's always funny
And never ever bad!

TONGUE TWISTERS

Tall tales told twist truth terribly!

* * * * * * * * *

Pairs of fairies share their chairs!

* * * * * * * * *

Pippa pickles potty pineapples pleasantly!

* * * * * * * * *

Exits and entrances for elephants are extra-enormous!

OUR GHOST IS VERY POLITE

Our ghost is very polite
He plays games in the middle of the night
Sometimes when I hear him sneeze
He always says 'Excuse me please!'

When I first met him he looked so sad
Then he noticed me and became very glad
'Delighted to see you, how-do-you-do!'
No one believes me but it's really true.

He watches the tele
He climbs on my bike
He walks on the ceiling every night!

SIX WEEKS

The magic of a summer day
Is but a memory to serve
The mind with picnics
Lingering days in the park
And shopping with Mum
For uniform.

Six weeks, some of which
Is a lazy dance with time,
Sleeping in and phoning friends
Playing in the garden
Of our imaginations leading
Into different lands.

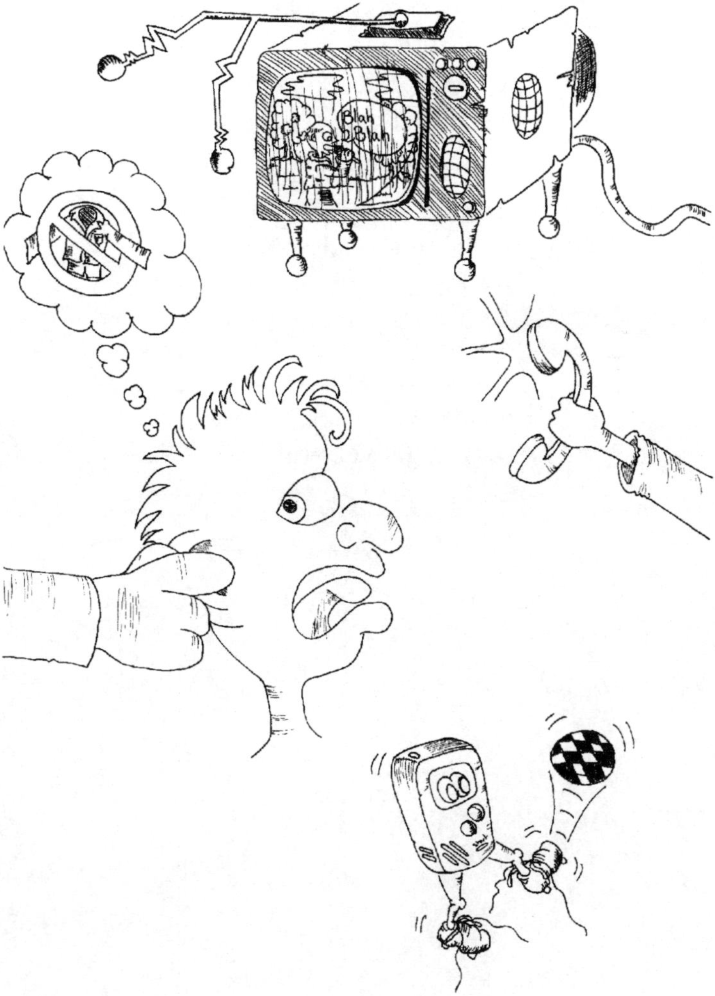
Blah
Blah

IF I WERE AT THE SEASIDE . . .

If I were at the seaside
I'd turn into a crab
I'd walk along sideways
And go dibadabdab.

If I were at the seaside
I'd be an ice-cream
I'd drip down Grandma's jumper
And make her scream.

If I were at the seaside
I'd build a sand castle
I'd eat lots of candy-floss
And get very full.

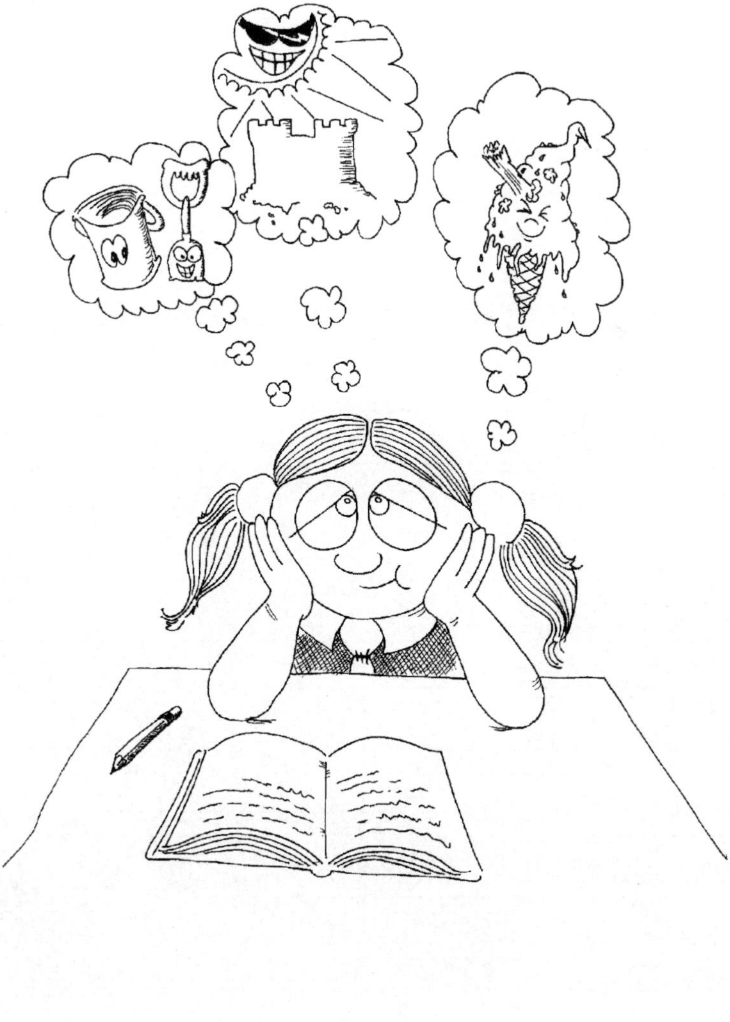

PERCY AND THE PIRATES

P ercy was swimming
I n the sea
R ound and round
A s happy as could be
T ill pirates saw him
E ating his tea!
S aid Percy . . . 'Goodbyeeee!'

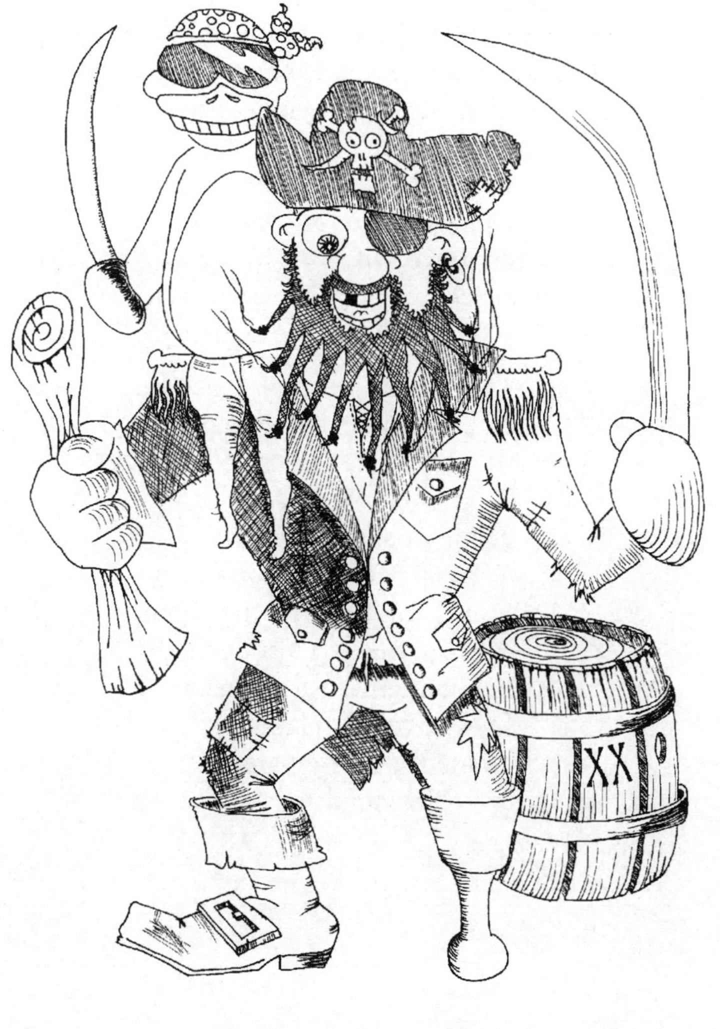
XX

PERCY IN THE WASHING MACHINE!

When Percy went to the nursery
And got sand all down his tummy
He had a chocolate biscuit and looked very funny
For the chocolate made some patterns
While he was playing there
And when he sploshed in puddles
All the children stood and stared!
He painted a lovely rainbow
And looked like one himself
The teacher nearly displayed him
In the middle of the shelf!

He went into the washing machine
Making noises as he spun
And told some silly stories
Until the wash was done:
Dingly-dangly creatures
Were dancing all around
And dinosaurs came up the pipes
Without making a sound.
Then that great big monster
Covered in hair
Made little Percy giggle
Inside there!

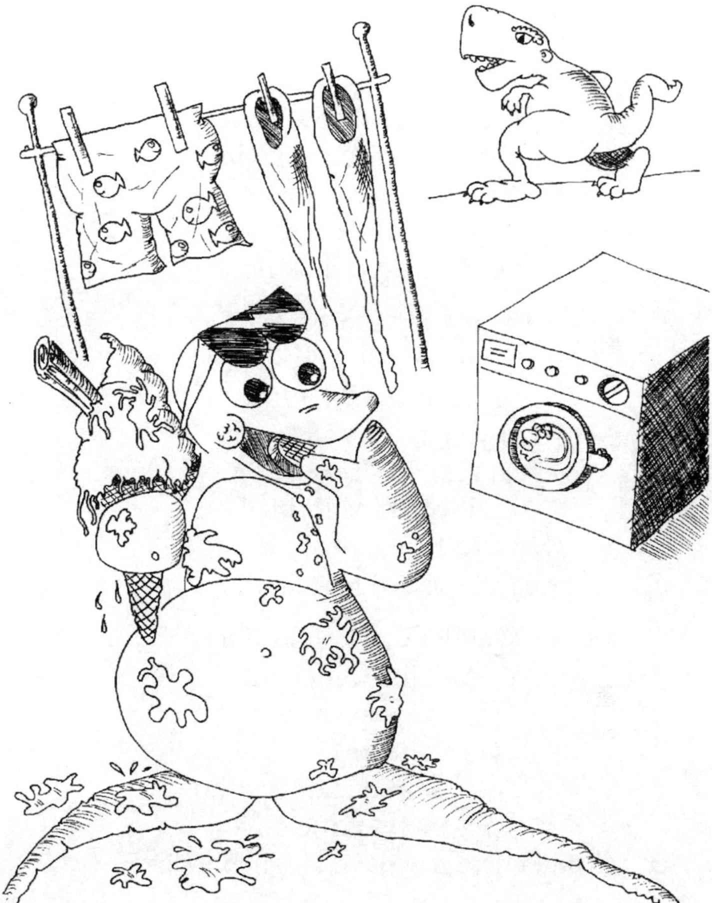

PERCY AND POPSY

When Percy met Popsy
It was at a dance
He was bopping about
Then suddenly by chance
This beautiful penguin
He'd not seen before
Appeared like a dream
On the busy dance-floor.

Then Percy approached her
And bowed very low
And asked so politely
'Will you dance with me now?'
'Oh yes,' said sweet Popsy,
'I would be thrilled
To be your partner'
And she kissed him on the bill!

Well Percy was blushing
And full of delight
To have such a partner
On Valentine's night!
And they danced and they flipped
Like sweet turtle doves
And Percy knew he had fallen in love.

WILL YOU . . . ?

'Will you personify me?'
Asked the tree.
The child replied
'It depends what kind of tree
You happen to be
As to how
I speak of you.'

Well, if I be
The Major Oak of Sherwood,
Sheltering Robin
From Sheriff-storms
How then
Would you
Tell of me?'

'You would be
The great-great grandfather
Of the forest -
Wise, wrinkled, gnarled;
An old storyteller
With a round
Big cellar.'

'If I were a beech or elm,
Maple or larch,
Pine or vine,
Would I be
Different and unique like you?
If I were a willow weeping
What would you do?'

If you were
The willow by the river,
Weeping your leaf-tears
Into the water,
I would listen to your tales
And touch your branches
Like a friend.'

FRIED EGGS AND JAM

I've come to sing to you
Hoping to bring to you
Stories to share with you and
FRIED EGGS AND JAM

Chorus

Playtime's for smiling and
Playtime's for laughing and
Playtime's for sharing and
FRIED EGGS AND JAM

Chorus

Pictures for looking at
Pictures for thinking about
Pictures for sharing and
FRIED EGGS AND JAM

Chorus

Stories for listening and
Stories for living and
Stories for sharing and
FRIED EGGS AND JAM

Chorus

IN AUGUST!

The cat glibbled its way across the carpet . . .
It was on a grey August day.
The cat was glibbling on its way
Till it decided to foddle and play
Bondoozling the budgie in its cage
So that the dog began to rage
And pomflicated the cat for that!
The cat jumped in Grandma's hat
Then poofled the guinea pig who'd been asleep!
Why, oh why did the cat go sleep?!
But there we are . . . it just goes to show
These things happen in August as you know!

THERE ARE ALIENS IN MY CLASSROOM

There are aliens in my classroom
Climbing up the walls
They've got two legs and a great big head
And they never come through the door!

There's aliens in the playground
Trying to catch the ball
Some are small, some very round
And some are very tall.

There's aliens eating sandwiches
There's aliens eating toast
Some are fond of chocolate cake
But it's crisps they like the most!

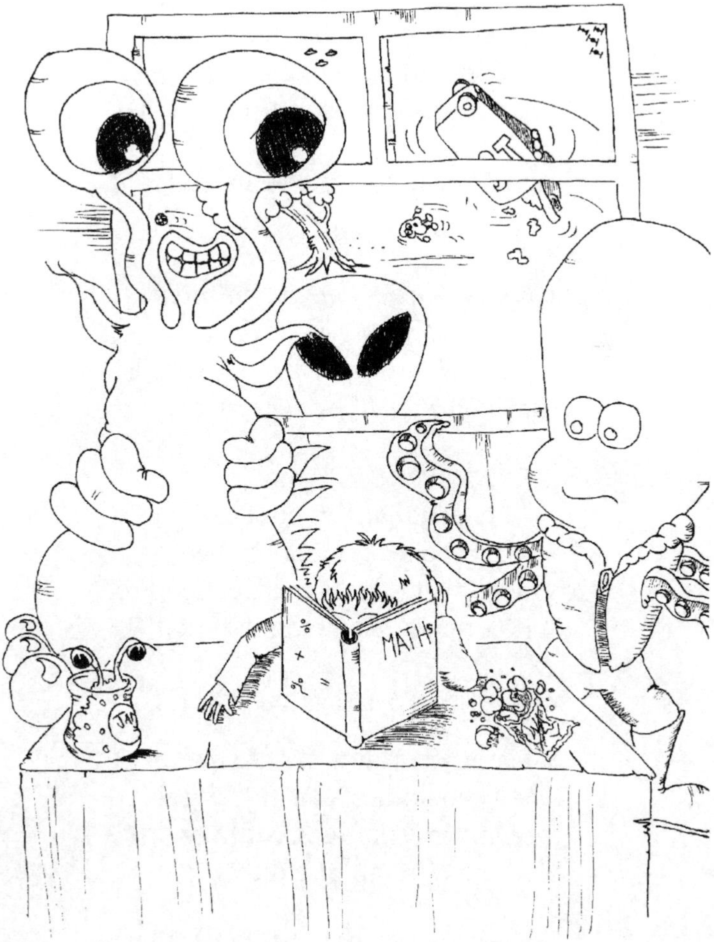
MATHS

THERE ARE THINGS IN MY ROOM AT NIGHT

When day has turned to night
And Mum puts out the light
I sometimes get a fright
When the shadows don't seem right.

Scream! Scream! Scream!

* * * * * * * * *

Chorus: They come out at night
And they sleep all day
There are things in my room at night
And I think they're here to stay!

* * * * * * * * *

I check that I'm not dead
Then I check under my bed
'Cos there's a monster there called Fred
Who often bops me on the head!

Scream! Scream! Scream!

When my curtains start to quiver
My bedclothes start to shiver
And I'm silly lump of liver
'Cos I'm all of a dither!

Scream! Scream! Scream!

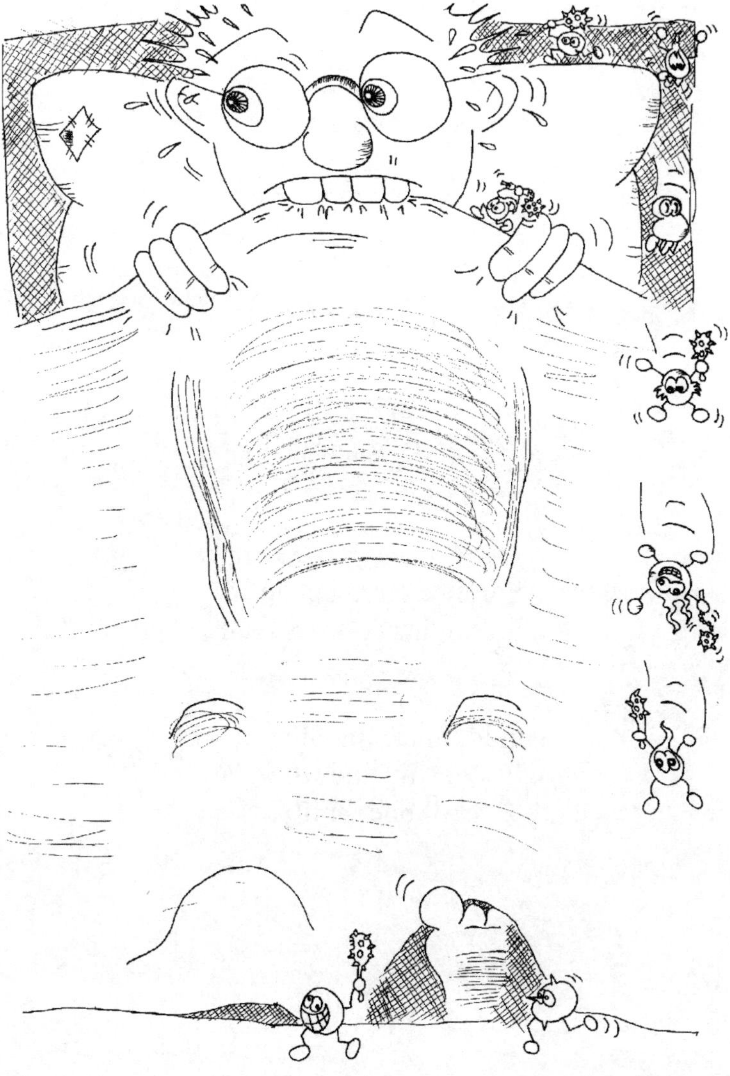

LIGHT HAIKUS

Candles being lit
On a special cake for me
It is my birthday.

* * * * * * * * *

Diwali is here
Houses are clean with welcome
Lakshmi is coming.

* * * * * * * * *

As sun descends, mother
Lights two candles for Shabbat.
For us, it's joyful.

* * * * * * * * *

At Advent we prepare
For the coming of Jesus.
Four lights on the wreath.

* * * * * * * * *

Hindu, Sikh, Buddhist, Jain,
Jew, Muslim and Christian -
All one family.

* * * * * * * * *

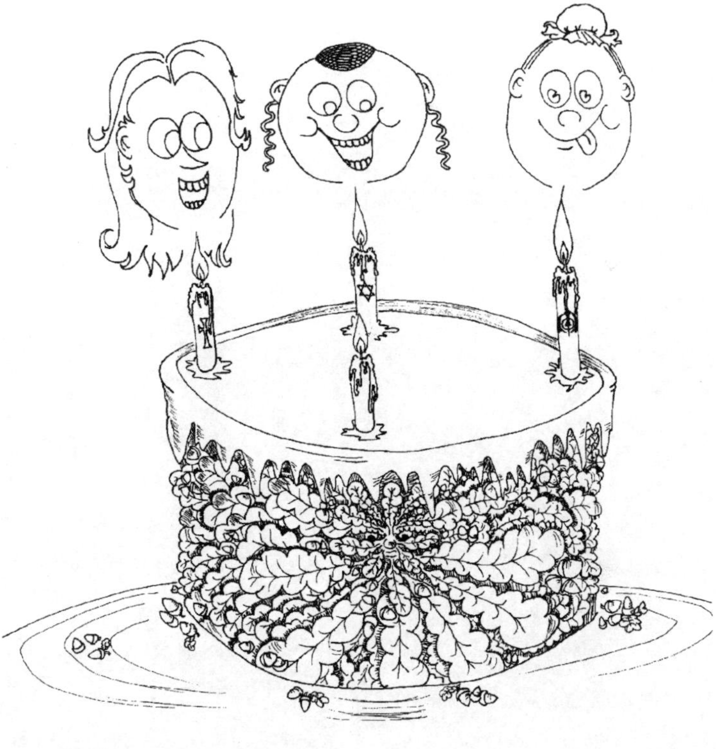